INSIDE**OUT**

INSIDE OUT

DANIELA SANTOS QUARTINO

BEVERLY MASSACHUSETTS

ROCKPORT
PUBLISHERS

A VISUAL TOUR OF OUTDOOR KITCHENS, GARDEN LIVING ROOMS, AND MORE

Copyright © 2008 by LOFT Publications

First published in the United States of America by
Rockport Publishers, a member of
Quayside Publishing Group
100 Cummings Center, Suite 406L
Beverly, MA 01915
Telephone: (978) 282-9590
Fax: (978) 283-2742
www.rockpub.com

ISBN-13: 978-1-59253-506-4
ISBN-10: 1-59253-506-2

Editor:
Daniela Santos Quartino

Text:
Bridget Vranckx and Daniela Santos Quartino

Art Director:
Mireia Casanovas Soley

Layout:
Esperanza Escudero Pino

Editorial project:
2008 © LOFT Publications
Via Laietana, 32, 4th, Of. 92
08003 Barcelona, Spain
Tel.: +34 932 688 088
Fax: +34 932 687 073
loft@loftpublications.com
www.loftpublications.com

Printed in China

CONTENTS

INTRODUCTION

When the square footage destined for the private home starts diminishing, people tend to feel the need to make the most of every inch of their house in order to improve their quality of living. Recent years are proof of this tendency, with a noticeable increase in the popularity of open-air spaces. According to a survey carried out by the American Institute of Architects, two thirds of professionals say they have noted an increase in the demand of open-air kitchens, patios, and decks.

This tendency is also clearly linked to the celebration of nature brought about by an environmental consciousness and a need for a stronger connection with one's surroundings. Nowadays people are no longer interested in merely sunbathing, they also want their daily activities to be outdoors to make the most of the fresh air, natural light, and views. If the weather conditions allow it, it no longer makes any sense to retreat to a closed room. Contemporary living conditions impose a need for drastic change after office hours and to be in environments that are radically different from one's work environment.

Moreover, the design industry has found a new niche in the rise of exterior spaces. Many household names, including Philippe Starck, Marcel Wanders, and Patricia Urquiola, are now turning their talents to the design of quality outdoor furniture, applying the latest technological innovations to create weather-resistant materials. Furthermore, exterior furnishings are not limited to furniture and decorative accessories, they extend to flat-screen televisions, music equipment, and electrical appliances designed to resist the sun and rain. This tendency represents a challenge for interior designers who must familiarize themselves with the language of landscape design, the microclimates of urban rooftops and the environmental particularities of each region.

The chapters of this volume will present the reader with a variety of examples of outdoor living, including kitchens, areas to relax, spas, bedrooms, dining rooms and spaces inspired by exotic cultures. The possibilities of opening up to the exterior are infinite.

Water-resistant mattresses, waterproof and fireproof fabrics, highly resistant teak wood, metal fabrics, and synthetic resins and fibers are designed to combat the effects of climate and allow bedrooms and chill out areas to be taken out of the home and into the open air.

The furniture itself defines these spaces, often characterized by over-sized proportions, appealing textures, and an abundance of cushions and mattresses to fall into.

Open-air chill out spaces easily adapt to the tastes and needs of the owners of a house: if they are placed in front of a large projection screen, for example, they become open-air movie theaters; placed underneath a pergola on a terrace, a space that would normally have limited use is transformed into a space that can be used all-year round.

This category includes outdoor bedrooms, which are not meant for outdoor sleeping, though can sometimes serve as guest bedrooms. Tree houses, for example, are ideal for those not only in search of close contact with nature, but also eager to comply with sustainable construction solutions. Canopy beds or Arab-style tents, on the other hand, are an ideal option for protection against the sun or evening dew, while portable fireplaces and outdoor fire pits transform the outdoors into a livable space during the winter months. All of these outdoor spaces provide an ideal setting for a moonlight *rendez-vous* any time of the year.

CHAPTER

1

Chill Out

Iporanga

This spectacular beach house sits on Iporanga Beach, an exclusive spot in a bay close to the village of Guarujá, between Sao Paulo and Rio de Janeiro. The owners, a family of Middle-Eastern origin living in New York, wanted the house to merge with the lush exterior and the adjacent sea and sand. A generous porch overlooks the garden, pool, beach, and ocean, while a rectangular swimming pool with canopied lounging area, separates the house from the beach and creates an interesting visual effect, artificially extending the image of the ocean.

p. 12-13 A comfortable lounge area overlooks the outdoor pool, the Atlantic Ocean, and Iporanga Beach situated in a natural reserve with waterfalls and lush exotic plants.

p. 14 A rectangular pool with a wooden platform on one end and a canopied beach lounge on the other end separates the beach from the house.

p. 15 Despite the straight and modern lines of this beach house, the place exudes a stylish, modern, and homely atmosphere and is ideal for leisure and entertaining, both inside and out.

Isay Weinfeld Iporanga Beach, Brazil © Reto Guntli/zapaimages.com

Cachagua House

Situated in a eucalyptus and pine tree forest, this contemporary weekend home on the central Chilean coast is inspired by some of the seaside resort's typical belle époque elements, such as pressure-treated pine and steel, with windows made of Tepa wood and stone. Two large terraces run the length of both façades and are perfect places to spend time with family and friends. Two trees are part of the side gallery and are central to the decoration. Discreet furniture adds a chic touch to the sober and contemporary architecture.

p. 21 Large terraces surround this weekend house and provide a kind of buffer between the home and the surrounding landscape. The decoration is in line with the purity of the architecture and the forest.

Isabel Trust

This mid-twentieth century residence located in the Trusdale Estates area of Beverly Hills underwent major renovation to update it to the twenty-first century. Without losing the spirit and character of the original building, the house was opened up to the views of Century City and several outdoor living spaces were created around the pool area. A canopy along the living room façade was removed to create a continuous ceiling plane that connects the interior and exterior spaces. Terrazzo flooring extends from some rooms to the exterior terraces, blurring the indoor and outdoor living spaces.

p. 23 Palos Verdes stone walls on the interior and exterior wall surfaces increase the blurred indoor and outdoor living spaces.

p. 24-25 Ample outdoor dining and living space is created around a pool in a Beverly Hills residence overlooking Century City.

Skyline Residence

This 5,800 sq ft (539 sq m) residence, which includes the main house and a guest house, is perched atop a ridgeline in the Hollywood Hills. The narrow and linear nature of the site encouraged a layout in which each room has at least one fully glazed wall to capitalize on transparency, reflections, and views. The South Wall of the guest house is used as a projection screen viewed from the roof deck above the garage.

p. 27 An outdoor chill out area is ideal for summer lounging, for contemplating the surrounding views and for watching movies projected on the wall above.

p. 28-29 An infinity pool brings the edge of the valley closer to the home and enhances the vastness and immediacy of the city below.

p. 30 The spatial relationship between form and view became paramount in the design and resulted in architecture that is complemented by its surroundings.

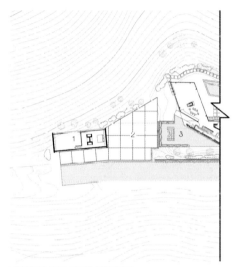
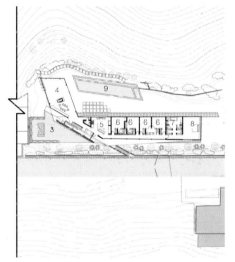

Floor plan: Guest House & Main House

1. Two story Guest House + Car port
2. Auto court / Otdoor movie seating
3. Outdoor viewing deck + Garage below
4. Living room / Dining room
5. Kitchen
6. Guest room
7. Master bathroom
8. Master bedrooom
9. Infinity edge pool

Between Alder and Oak

This tree house in a small town in northern Germany serves as a room for rest and relaxation as well as a guestroom and outdoor dining area. A first set of stairs leads up to a spacious terrace, large enough for a table and chairs. A second set of stairs leads up to a cabin with a curved roof fitted with glazing on all sides and a large dormer window. The surrounding landscape can be enjoyed from a spacious lounge area inside the cabin. At night, the lit-up structure is visible from a great distance.

p. 35 Drawers situated underneath a bed with a bench at the end, provide plenty of storage space

Baumraum   Bad Rothenfelde, Germany   © Dirk Vogel

Magic Box Inc

This transparent and highly versatile 'box' changes the stereotypes of prefabricated houses and extension rooms. Its concept is based on a fusion of art and architecture and its goal is to provide a type of space that has never been experienced before. The box can be used as a working space, hobby room, café, spa or anything else you can imagine in any desired size. It is made with water-resistant materials and can be installed in a very short period of time.

p. 37 This "magic box" can be installed on a flat surface, on a slope, or even on a rooftop. The surface area of the glass is customized depending on the use, location, and weather.

p. 38 This box has secure and tempered windows for security and safety reasons. The structure is made of steel or stainless steel and is painted in the client's chosen color.

Gallery

∧ Outdoor furniture is no longer limited to common deck chairs, plastic furnishings or foldable tables. Nowadays, an outdoor living room is much like the interior version.

< Outdoor fire pits add a touch of romance to open-air entertaining and provide warmth on those cool summer and winter nights.

∧ A series of wooden platforms with mattresses and cushions covered in white sailcloth create a perfect private chill out area.

∧ Candles and lanterns scattered throughout the property create a medieval,
magical ambience.

∧ A pergola with drapes not only provides a shaded and cool area to relax during the day, but also adds life and an element of fun to any urban terrace.

> An outdoor living and dining area adds to the quality of urban life, allowing city dwellers to escape their frenetic lifestyles without having to leave their beloved cities.

∧ Over-sized elements are a typical feature of outdoor living areas: add a holiday atmosphere to a dull urban rooftop terrace with an over-sized lounger and some parasols.

< To maintain the natural, unforced look of a garden, add simple furniture that blends in with its surroundings, like this simple hanging structure, reminiscent of a beehive.

An open fire makes sure an outdoor living area inspired by the surrounding countryside can be enjoyed all year round.

∧ The original structure of this rustic building was used to create outdoor
seating areas, enlivened with a typical country décor.

∧ Thanks to new technological innovations and a wide selection of outdoor furniture, open-air living rooms are now popping up on urban rooftops all over the world.

> A simple rug, some cushions, and a small table covered by an Arabian-style canopy create the perfect setting for an informal chill out area in a rural setting.

Accessories Gallery

© Gandia Blasco

© Marcel Wanders

© Jane Hamley Wells

© Jane Hamley Wells

© Garda

© Viteo

© Philippe Starck/Sutherland

© Extremis

© Gandia Blasco

© Philippe Starck/Sutherland

© Extremis

© Habitat

Simple and rural or complex and refined, outdoor kitchens take the everyday act of cooking and eating to a new level, giving it an almost festive quality influenced by the surroundings and the climate. The design of the outdoor kitchen is defined by the shape of the island: simple, U-shaped, or L-shaped. The grill, sink, and work surface are fundamental elements of these spaces.

The most complete outdoor kitchens include fridges, freezers, ice machines and larders. Sometimes they extend to worktops or eating surfaces and are complemented with tables and chairs that are part of an adjacent dining room.

The flooring surrounding these spaces must be made of porous materials to avoid accidents that can be caused by water or grease.

Independent and mobile islands are an ideal solution for large spaces where a kitchen can be installed quickly in a garden or on a rooftop.

Stone ovens or fixed barbecues, on the other hand, require very little maintenance and do not easily wear out. They can also be turned into wood-burning fires during the colder months of the year.

Cooking & Dining

2

2inns

The main aim of this project is to capture the beautiful Southern California weather and unobstructed views of La Jolla. The project explores the spatial qualities of a continuous interior-exterior space within the private realms of two identical, adjacent houses. The main level is elevated from the street and enclosed by twenty-five glass panels. These panels can slide open on an automated track to create a continuous open plane, connecting the back garden to the ocean views and transforming the kitchen, living and dining areas into complete exterior spaces.

p. 60-61 An outdoor fire adds a touch of romanticism to the exterior dining experience, created by opening up the twenty-five full height glass panels surrounding the main level.

p. 64 The two adjacent houses are set back from the street and are carved into the existing topography.

59

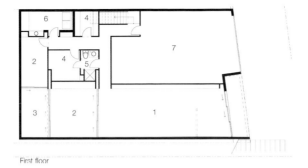

First floor

1. Playroom
2. Office
3. Patio
4. Cellar
5. Bathroom
6. Laundry
7. Parking

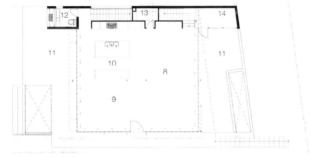

Basement

8. Livingroom
9. Diningroom
10. Kitchen
11. Terrace
12. Bathroom
13. Storage
14. Cellar

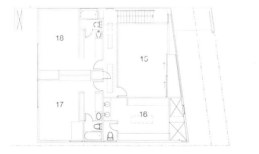

Second floor

15. Main bedroom
16. Main bathroom
17. Bedroom
18. Bedroom

Bridge House

Situated on fifteen acres of wooded grasslands, this house runs east to west, bridging a ravine that runs through the site. The living areas on the upper level have continuous glass walls that face north towards the hills. The bedrooms on the lower level face south and are also surrounded by glass walls. A deck on the upper bridge serves as an outdoor dining space and also links the entrance to the house on one side to the entrance to the pool and guest house on the other. The deck also connects to paths that lead into the landscape.

p. 68 The walls and roof of this house are clad in plates of corten steel. Viewed from above, the rusty bar creates an interesting contrast with the golden grass slopes.

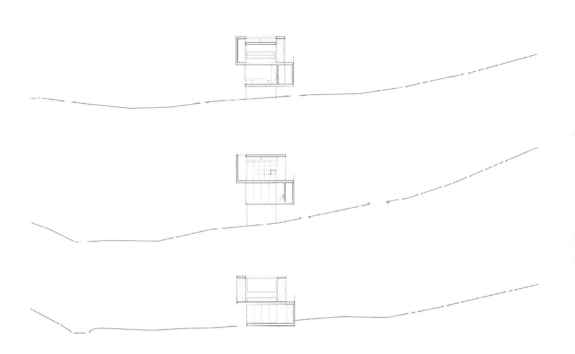

Cross Sections

Calming Retreat in California

This garden, situated in a district in the San Fernando Valley of the city of Los Angeles, was created as an outdoor entertaining space for friends and clients. The garden, with its evergreens and perennials of dark green, silver and chartreuse, is a calming retreat from the city. A lime-peal-colored steel trellis conceals the outdoor lighting and heaters and also provides an overhead structure for evergreen grape vines above the dining terrace. Minimalist concrete bowls, which are situated at opposite ends of the garden, serve as an outdoor fire pit and a water element.

p. 72 A selection of evergreens and perennials create the perfect backdrop for outdoor dining. The dining area is made of honed bluestone paving and Ipe decking.

p. 73 A barbecue is placed in such a way as to encourage interaction between guests and the chef. Moreover, the honed bluestone barbecue top acts as a table for serving the meals.

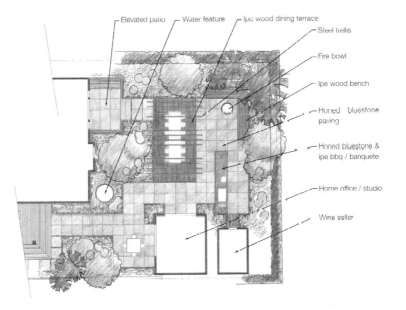

Elevated patio — Water feature — Ipe wood dining terrace

Steel trellis

Fire bowl

Ipe wood bench

Honed bluestone paving

Honed bluestone & ipe bbq / banquete

Home office / studio

Wine cellar

Six

Six is a Southern California housing scheme that combines clear form with continuous indoor/outdoor spaces. Situated on a sloping lot on a curving street, the six town residences that make up this project create a visual rhythm of contrasting volumes and projecting balconies extending towards the ocean. Fold-away glass doors that open completely at both ends of a loft-like space contain the kitchen, living, and dining room. They also serve to connect this main living space with the front and back gardens to create a continuous outdoor experience.

p. 78 The connection between the interior and exterior is made seamless by fold-away full height glass doors and Ipe flooring, which runs outside as decking.

Sebastian Mariscal Studio   San Diego, CA, USA   © Hisao Suzuki

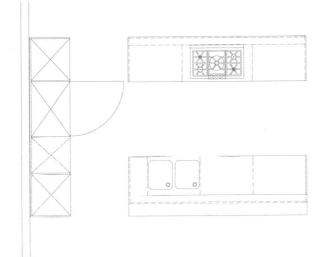

Floor Plan

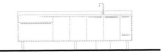

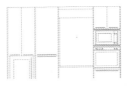

Cross Sections

Princess Margaret

The owner of this private garden in Toronto, Canada, wanted a visual attraction in the backyard that would also fuction as a reading nook with visibility in all directions and a place to sit, relax, and eat. The result is this modern gazebo, a wooden structure partly framed on all sides with pieces of opaque glass. The structure is lit at night and adds a romantic element to the garden after dusk.

 p. 82-83 Colorful planters placed along the path leading to the casual outdoor living area blend in with the lush natural landscape of this backyard.

Gallery

∧ An outdoor stone oven is ideal not only for barbecues in the summer but also for an outdoor open fire on cooler winter nights.

< An outdoor grill with an incorporated seating area is the main feature of the patio of this Californian home.

∧ Spectacular scenery can be enjoyed from the deck of this house in a coastal town of Uruguay even while preparing the grill.

< The cooking area is the central feature of this outdoor dining and kitchen space, made with locally sourced materials.

△ This luxury rooftop garden one hundred feet above Chicago's famed "Magnificent Mile" is inspired by views of Midwest agricultural landscape.

< Letting nature run wild in your outdoor dining room will not only create a pleasant environment, but will also provide shade during the hottest hours of the day.

∧ A huge white canvas offers protection from the sun and rain.

> This bar, which could easily be an indoor feature, proves that indoor and outdoor are now practically interchangeable.

∧ Outdoor lighting now comes in all shapes and sizes and is inspired by indoor illumination.

< This orient-inspired open fire creates the perfect mood for a romantic evening meal.

∧ Be inspired by the traditional picnic: choose your favorite spot under a tree and set up your outdoor living and dining space.

> You don't need to wait until you go on that exotic vacation to create your own enchanting holiday setting: a few candles, mood lighting, and light fabrics will do the trick.

∧ This kitchen is ideally placed in between both an indoor and an outdoor dining area, and beneath a glass canopy.

< A modern kitchen sits on the border between the interior and the exterior. The indoor dining area has a glass ceiling, which creates the illusion of outdoor dining.

Accessories Gallery

© Gandia Blasco

© Garpa

© Extremis

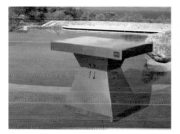

© Kalamzo

© Jane Hawley Wello

© Gervasoni

© Gervasoni

© Grapa

© Conmoto

© Radius

© Conmoto

© Emme group

© Halamazoo

© Linx Professional Grills

© Radius

© Vitôô

© Linx Professional Grills

© Jane Hawley Wells

The increasing popularity of spas is a phenomenon which experts believe will become even more pronounced and enter new territories. Gardens and patios of modern homes are one of the most prolific new settings being turned into true temples of relaxation and health treatments, thanks to an increasingly wide array of specialized equipment available at ever-decreasing costs.

Depending on one's budget, a private home spa can mean taking a bath out of its normal indoor setting and placing it outside, inviting residents and guests alike to take long soaking hydro-massage baths or Jacuzzis.

A private outdoor spa can be complemented by a shower with stimulating water jets, which are available in a wide variety, including jets that simulate tropical rain and devices that emit relaxing aromas to create a marine, flower or meadow ambience.

Some outdoor spas include a space to work out or do yoga, and are equipped with areas that contain simple furniture in neutral colors, like the best professional spas.

Similar to indoor spas, these outdoor spaces can be used both in the summer and in the winter. The latter have one advantage: when it is freezing outside, one can experience a natural shock therapy induced by the contrast between hot and cold.

3

Spas

Hidden Paradise

The Argentine architect who designed this summer house was given *carte blanche* by the young Italian couple who spend their summers in this idyllic place. Their only request was a home that reminds them of Morocco. The result is a spectacular space with theatrical elements, such as a canopy bed and old bronze bath tub with shower head, located a few feet away from the entrance, as well as a cement deck and series of lounge chairs.

p. 107 An old bronze bath tub surrounded by wooden panels is placed only a few feet away from the pergola that protects the cars from the intense summer sun.

p. 111 The gallery, which looks onto the infinity pool, is divided into two areas: on one side is the outdoor hearth and on the other is an area for relaxing with two comfortable sofas.

Diego Montero   Punta del Este, Uruguay   © Juan Hitters/surpressagencia.com

Emmerson Sauna

Inspired by the constructions built by the original Finnish settlers upon their arrival in the United States, this large, freestanding building is designed to house a sauna and to hold social gatherings, a practice associated to this bathing ritual that has long since disappeared. As cooling is an important part of this custom, the building is equipped with an outdoor shower and triangular seating area, designed to let a gentle breeze pass through. The traditional materials used for this building—brick and wood—not only maintain the heat, but also create a warm and welcoming environment.

p. 113 Despite its contemporary look and technical innovations, this spa still manages to evoke the spirit of the traditional Finnish sauna.

Wood Appeal

This two-story vacation home in an ultra-chic beach resort of Uruguay is surrounded by a forest of pine trees. The domestic layout has been inverted so the residents can enjoy the views over the ocean as much as possible: bedrooms are placed on the first floor, while a big area for socializing, surrounded by large exterior galleries, takes up the second floor. To make the most of the outdoors and the views of the sea and the forest, the galleries contain a second living and dining area, as well as an outdoor shower.

p. 119 A simple, yet refined look is achieved through a balanced mix of oriental textiles and decorative elements with contemporary designer pieces of furniture.

Venice Garden

This lush garden with a hot tub is an ideal resting place after a long, hard day at work. The hot tub comes with a small seating area for relaxing and is slightly secluded from the other outdoor spaces that include a dining and living area. A combination of natural colors and materials creates a very harmonious ambience: different tones of green, brown, and red blend in well with the natural materials of the furniture as well as the foliage surrounding this space.

p. 123 A long wooden table is ideal for outdoor summer dining. The green chairs combine well with the natural color of the wood.

Winter Residence

The transformation of this home began as a simple request for a bathroom remodel. The owners wanted to create bathrooms that reflected the minimal and contemplative feel of the modern spas and boutique hotels they had visited on their travels. To create this spa-like feel, the original kidney-shaped pool was replaced by a new blue glass-tiled and terrazzo-like plastered pool, with "floating" concrete bridges, which link the main deck to the master bedroom deck and linear outdoor fireplace.

p. 127 A 35 sq ft glass and tile shower addition on the east side of the house is surrounded by a tiny courtyard, which allows the bather to feel as though they are outside, yet out of view.

Dolomites House

The garden area of this house, located in the Dolomite mountain range on the border between Italy and Austria, is enclosed by an 8 ft tall wood wall with horizontal slats. The wall emphasizes the perspective and casts shadows of sunlight from above and of spotlights from below. The house is surrounded by a wooden deck, made of 5.5 in-wide Ipe wood planks, which runs up to a sunbathing platform with a Jacuzzi. The deck can be covered by a white canopy that runs on tracks inserted in steel beams and covers the length of the deck, so the owners can sit out on a rainy day.

p. 132 To ensure a maximum amount of light is let into the rooms, the façades have been replaced by a custom designed structural silicone curtain wall and large sliding glass doors.

p. 134 A wrap-around deck offers plenty of opportunities for outdoor lounging and entertaining even when it is raining, thanks to a white canopy, which covers the length of the deck.

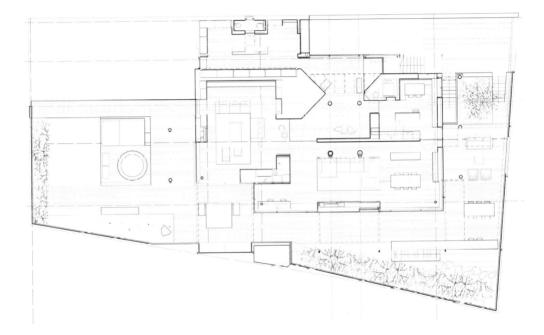

Ground floor plan

Bath on the rooftop

This 7'10" wide building has been converted into a luxury space for urban living. The only border with the outside is glass, making the interiors completely visible to the exterior world. Like a living painting and a nod to the former red light district, every floor is framed by black window frameworks. The street level is for working, the first level for eating, the second for living and the third for sleeping. As space is tight, even the rooftop has been used for a domestic activity: (sun)bathing.

p. 138 The architects and owners of this house cannot complain that they do not know their neighbors: by using the roof for their bathing, they are taking advantage of every bit of space.

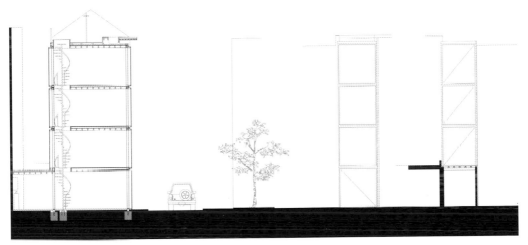

Cross Section

Gallery

∧ What better way to wind down after a stressful day or week of work than to immerse yourself in a bath and soak up the calm surrounding scenery?

< This private outdoor spa has been inspired by ethnic elements that add an exotic touch to an outdoor bathing space.

∧ A spa has become a common feature of many private outdoor living spaces.

< An outdoor Jacuzzi could be the perfect antidote to a stressful lifestyle.

∧ A white canvas awning can be adjusted to cover this outdoor spa area and create a more intimate and quiet ambience.

> A bath is embedded into a wooden floor in one of the patios of this house in Japan, where bathing is an important ritual linked to a person's well-being.

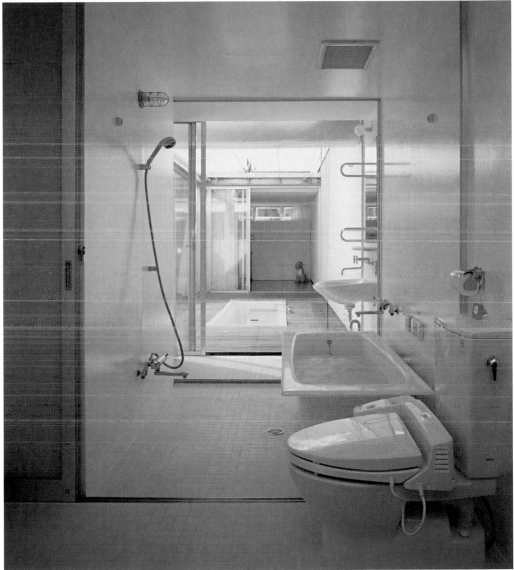

Accessories Gallery

© Jane Hamley Wells

© Jane Hamley Wells

© Gandia Blasco

© Habitat

© Gervasoni

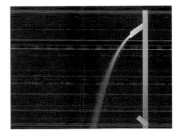

© Conmoto

Homes are being deconstructed so that they can be redesigned outside the limits of the supporting walls and out into the open air.

These settings are especially designed for the enjoyment of a cup of coffee or an informal meal, a place where one can listen to music, play, read, or socialize. There are as many possibilities as there are lifestyles, though there is one universal requisite: close contact with the environment—the feeling that you are in the front row of a daily show of privileged views of the city and the surrounding landscape or, if the property allows it, the simple hypnotic vision of a pool of water.

These outdoor living rooms can be independent constructions linked to the adjacent exterior spaces, such as porches or decks. They can also be completely open spaces, such as patios and gardens. The presence of large openings is fundamental, be it in the shape of arches, windows, or glass walls.

Furniture plays an important role in the definition of these living rooms and the rise of a variety of new materials has led to an increase in creative possibilities. Vanguard pieces of design, which look like indoor furniture, are adapted and made weather-resistant.

As a result, the traditional plastic sun lounger or foldable wooden table has made way for Chesterfield sofas, Louis XV armchairs, and twentieth-century designer chairs, accompanied by coffee tables, lamps, and decorative objects that further blur the limits between the interior and the exterior.

Living

Pool House

The idea behind this pool house (915 sq ft [85 sq m]) was to create a private urban oasis to which the owners could escape and enjoy "being on vacation" without having to leave the city. The 26' × 13' pool is the *raison d'être* of this pool house. The space is designed like a loft with a living and dining area that can be turned into a sleeping area when needed. This main space is completely opened up to the outside leaving the boundaries between the interior and the exterior blurred.

p. 151 The large white sofa doubles as a bed when needed and a large, gold-framed mirror behind the dining area reflects the pool and radiates light.

p. 153 Four concrete columns in the corner of the terrace support a pergola, which provides shade on the hottest days.

p. 154 Light furniture — a rattan and bamboo coffee table (painted white) and rattan chairs with white cushions — helps create a relaxed atmosphere in the pool house.

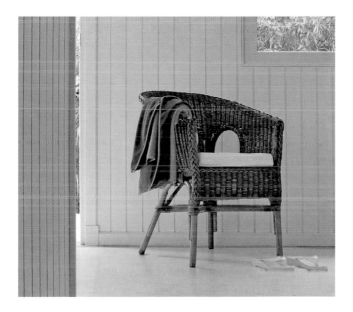

Mirindiba House

The design of this urban house, which combines dark Brazilian hardwood, concrete, and stone, is responsive to the climate of Brazil: walls and shades can be opened as necessary and the reflecting pools offer natural cooling. A thick stone wall is the structural and visual backbone of the house. An open-plan living room, situated on the ground floor, is completely open to the exterior. Huge sliding doors, which are hidden in the wall, allow it to be closed off or to extend out to the pool and deck area.

p. 156 The activities in the main living areas of this urban house in Brazil can easily flow out to the exterior, blurring the boundaries between interior and exterior.

p. 158 A reflecting pool offers natural cooling, an important feature in the Brazilian climate.

p. 159 This house is like a see-through box when all the windows and shutters are open, making it hard to distinguish interior and exterior living spaces.

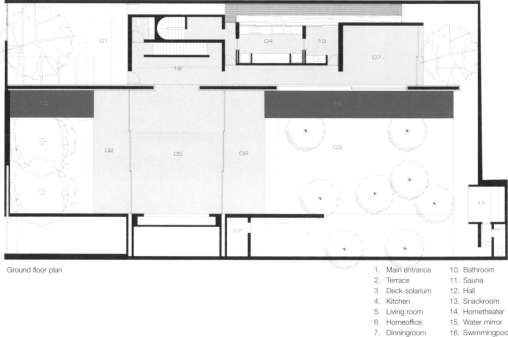

Ground floor plan

1. Main entrance
2. Terrace
3. Deck-solarium
4. Kitchen
5. Living room
6. Homeoffice
7. Dinningroom
8. Bedrooom
9. Closet
10. Bathroom
11. Sauna
12. Hall
13. Snackroom
14. Hometheater
15. Water mirror
16. Swimmingpool
17. Storage

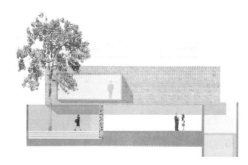

Cross Sections

161

Ixtapa House

This holiday home on a private beach on the Pacific Ocean was built for a large family. The design of the living area follows the traditional typology of the high *palapa* roofs of Mexican beach houses. However, in order to create a more intimate space, the columns supporting the roof were replaced by two organic volumes that close off the direct view from the inland. The classic structural tripartite floor-wall-ceiling is dissolved into one single gesture that embraces the space and frames the view of the ocean beyond.

p. 162 The open living space is made of plaster combined with plastic additives which enable the shell to expand and contract.

p. 164-165 Contemplation of the ocean and privacy were two of the main priorities in the design of this exterior living space.

p. 167 Though the communal area is large enough to receive many guests, the space maintains an intimate and protected feeling.

First Floor

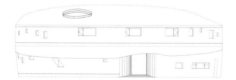

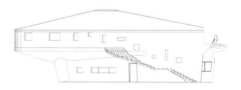

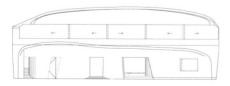

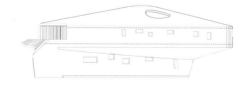

Cross Sections

Wilton Pool House

Part of a 3.5 acre property in Connecticut, the minimalist architecture of this pool house contrasts with the traditional architecture of the existing house. Hovering over a 48' × 20' pool like a vessel in the water, this 1,200 sq ft structure contains a spa and indoor/outdoor shower. The roofed veranda acts as an indoor/outdoor dining area with a large opening in the wall that frames the landscape beyond. The area around the pool, paved in travertine with steps and walls of stone, becomes a sunken courtyard.

p. 169 A fire pit on the south side of the structure adds an intimate quality to the space and is an ideal spot for gathering on cooler nights.

p. 170 The interior of the house is enclosed by a series of metal and glass sliding panels, which give the structure a transparent quality and allow the interior to blend with the exterior.

p. 176-177 The main frame and ceiling of this minimalist structure are made of Ipe wood and give the place a warm, nautical, and sculptural touch.

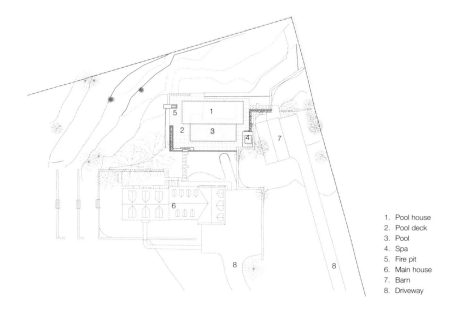

1. Pool house
2. Pool deck
3. Pool
4. Spa
5. Fire pit
6. Main house
7. Barn
8. Driveway

Floor Plans

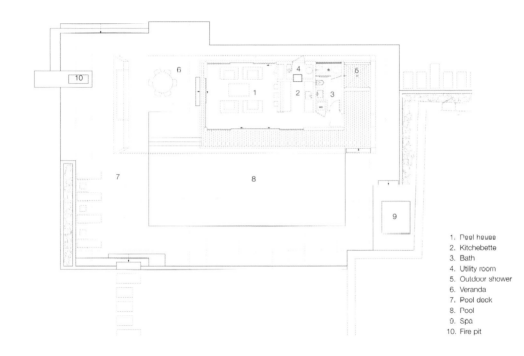

1. Pool house
2. Kitchebette
3. Bath
4. Utility room
5. Outdoor shower
6. Veranda
7. Pool deck
8. Pool
9. Spa
10. Fire pit

Villa Soravia

This luxurious vacation home lies on the shore of Lake Millstatt at the southernmost tip of Millstatt, a health resort in Carinthia, Austria. The lower area has semi-public, transparent rooms. The living room on this same level has floor-to-ceiling windows that can be completely opened so the interior and exterior spaces flow together. A terrace extends the interior living room out towards the lake, while a small living area has been created in one of the corners next to this space. Sicilian olive trees, both inside and outside, add a Mediterranean flair.

 p. 181 A cedar-wood pavilion juts out over the lake on an elevated walkway. A swing is attached to the underside of the platform.

This tree house in a large private garden serves as a playground, a room for rest and relaxation, and even a place to hold a business meeting. A staircase leads up to the first, spacious terrace, which has an outdoor shower and is large enough for a table and a few chairs. More steps lead about three feet higher up to a cabin. The interior is furnished with high-quality benches on all three sides and a small table. There is plenty of storage space as well as a stereo system and large dormer window. Artificial lighting and heating ensure this space is comfortable for use all year round.

p. 185 Surrounded by nature, a tree house offers an ideal escape from the hustle and bustle of city living.

p. 187 A tatajuba terrace and tree house are supported by two high-grade steel frames, lifting this living space some 13 ft off the ground.

King Henry's Road

The architects have played with the idea of invisibility to create an interior space with an exterior feel. There are no columns or fins for this structure. The simple walls act as cantilevers to support the roof, which is a single sheet of glass supported by the thinnest of glass beams. Gaps in the floor slates allow for air to be pumped in, while high level vents in the brick wall pull air out, thus keeping the space at external temperatures in summer. During the cooler months, the space is kept warm through a heating system under the floor.

p. 190 The addition can be separated from the rest of the flat by means of two simple sliding glass doors.

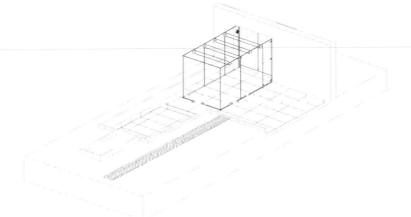

Axonometry

1. Two sheets of 12 mm toughened and heat soaked glass laminated together with clear resin interlock
2. 10 mm ventilation gaps in between flooring slabs
3. Removable aluminium panels
4. Existing brickwork
5. 3 mm s/s angle
6. Brushes
7. 3 mm s/s cover to mdf
8. Dorma rs 120 sliding door track with 10 mm toughened glass
9. Holes in slabs to lock door into place
10. Extract pipe
11. Rendered reveal
12. 8 mm glass door with dorma double hinge
13. Drainage channel below slate
14. Air input vent connected to fan via network of deep pipes

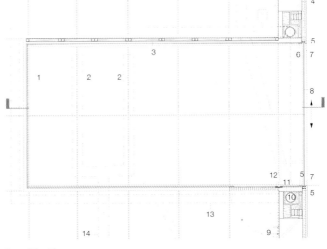

Ground Floor Plan

Maritime Refuge

This weekend home in the country not only provides views of the surrounding fields, but one can also catch a glimpse of the Atlantic Ocean on one side and the José Ignacio lagoon on the other. The owners wanted a warm, fun, and informal place where the whole family could rest. The house is surrounded by patios and decks, which are used as extended living areas: a wooden deck chair covered with a cream-colored canvas is a perfect place for solitary reading, and an open fire made of the same stone as the exterior walls prepares the residents for outdoor living during the cold winters.

p. 193 A comfortable outdoor living area with wine-colored awnings overlooks a refreshing pool with an infinite border.

Beaver Street Reprise

The top floor of this modern house in a Victorian neighborhood of San Francisco consists of a split-level living area and gallery kitchen that opens out onto a huge deck. The roof extends from the interior living space and covers a large portion of the deck to create a protected outdoor living room. Two sliding glass walls ensure continuity from the inside to the outside. A rotating fireplace, able to face the interior or exterior, is hung outside to further blur these boundaries.

p. 194 A fireplace hung outside can be turned to face the interior if necessary. The furniture of this residence is flexible and can be easily used inside or outside.

Gallery

∧ Mood lighting and a fireplace ensure residents can enjoy a relaxed atmosphere or casual dining experience in a loggia in the evenings throughout the
year.

< The covered loggia of this Italian villa is in keeping with the Tuscan style of
this home in Beverly Hills.

∧ Take your living room outside to make the most of the outdoors and reap
the benefits of being surrounded by nature all year round.

∧ Equip your outdoor living room with the same kind of comfortable furniture you would use indoors to enjoy the summer days and nights.

∧ A well-equipped outdoor living area can be turned into a guest bedroom if you run out of space inside.

< Pavilions are a traditional addition to many country homes and can be turned into flexible and fully-equipped living extensions.

∧ A variety of outdoor plants help bring you closer to nature and make outdoor entertaining more pleasant.

> Soft, neutral tones help blend a living area into the surroundings and create
a harmonious environment for outdoor living.

∧   A former tool shed, garage, or any other unused annex can be transformed
    into a private space close to nature, ideal for reading, entertaining, or relaxing.

>   Turn an outdoor living space into a place for work and let nature inspire you
    and your business meetings.

© Patrick Spence/Redcover

∧ Why sit indoors when you can enjoy all the creature comforts outside and relax at the edge of the pool in style?

< Even the smallest outdoor spaces can be turned into lush urban living areas with a variety of plants and some comfortable chairs.

Accessories Gallery

© Jane Hawley Wells

© Viteo

© Gervasoni

© Jane Hawley Wells

© Studio JSPR

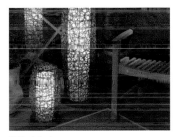

© Shady Lady

© Bonacina Pier Antonzo

© Garpa

© Studio JSPR

© Cervasoni

© Shady Lady

© Radius

Influenced by a favorable climate and cultural traditions, the gardens of the Middle East are designed for the senses and to accommodate a large number of daily activities.

Gazebos, tea houses, haimas, and pavilions are distributed throughout these beautiful, delicate, yet overwhelming gardens with fountains, footbridges, and ponds for fish and water plants.

These structures are usually made of very strong wood or highly-resistant materials to withstand humid and wet climates. They contain spaces for resting, eating, and entertaining and are closely connected to nature.

Some interesting architectural examples include gazebos situated at the edge of reflecting pools, typical of Thai culture, or Japanese tea houses at the end of gardens, reached only by a winding stone pathway.

In terms of decoration, it is important to keep in mind those details such as colorful mosaic tiles or tropical plants with very big, green leaves. Furniture made with natural fibers, chopped wood, vibrant colored textiles, oil lamps, sheer cloth, floor cushions and delicate parasols are ideal for these spaces.

Exotic

Balinese Garden

The garden of this urban Australian home was the main attraction for the relatively new owners. Despite the unpredictable Melbourne weather, the family of three spends a lot of time in their lush garden, which is laid out around a pool and divided into several zones. There are sitting areas at either side of the entry and at the end of the pool. A Balinese pavilion, furnished like an outdoor room with lounge chairs, a chest-cum coffee table, and even a sisal carpet, hovers over the swimming pool. The pavilion is one of the residents' favorite places for reading, for relaxing, and even for holding meetings.

p. 221 The Balinese pavilion and canvas umbrellas offer shade in the summer, while a terracotta Mexican outdoor fireplace ensures the garden can be used during the colder months.

p. 222-223 The Balinese pavilion at one end of the pool is furnished like an outdoor room with sofas, a coffee table, and even a rug.

p. 224 Tall palm trees create a shady canopy in this urban garden, which appears much bigger than it really is thanks to its division into several zones.

Somer Tea House

Micro compact home—or M-ch, for short—was developed from the "i-home" project, a light 8.5 ft cube conceived by architect Richard Horden and his students in Munich's Technological University. In terms of space usage M-ch draws on aeronautical and automobile design, while its scale and harmonies come from the architecture of the classic Japanese teahouse. Within its space of under 75 sq ft, this cube offers a place for each of the four basic requirements of a home: resting, working, eating, and washing. Inside this wooden and aluminum structure, the foldaway bed can be found above.

p. 231 Selective outdoor furniture creates a comfortable outdoor living room complete with fireplace.

Camp Howie House
Chiang Mai

This extensive garden is presented as a theme park composed of different spaces, each with their own character. A large number of bridges and gazebos, connected by stone paths, cross the garden closely connected to a large swimming pool and to a stream that practically surrounds the entire home. In some cases, the exhuberant tropical vegetation creates areas that seem to have come straight out of a fairy tale. Other micro gardens are equipped with fountains and furniture for relaxing or eating outdoors.

p. 234 The living spaces in the garden house a collection of bizarre objects that are typical of the region.

p. 238 The gazebos encourage stops along the trail to contemplate the scenaery.

p. 240-241 The guest pavilion occupies an important space in the garden, just outside of any central structures.

Gallery

∧ A selection of exotic parasols surrounding a pool set in lush surroundings
adds an instant exotic touch to an outdoor living space.

< Don't restrict an outdoor living space to one area, create a series of spaces
and add exotic elements to create a genuine tropical ambience.

∧ Place a mattress and matching cushions on your patio and while away the hours in your Moroccan-inspired lounge.

< Use natural tones to blend a relaxed outdoor living space in with its surroundings and create a harmonious living environment.

∧ Be inspired by the look of this lush and exotic garden in Thailand with a series of raised walkways that lead to an outdoor pavilion.

> Surround an exterior living space with an abundance of greenery and create an instant exotic look for outdoor living and entertaining.

Accessories Gallery

© Studio lilica

© Roche Bobois

© Habitat

© Gandia Blasco

© Roche Bobois

© Habitat

© Habitat

© Habitat

© Roche Bobois

© Habitat

© Habitat

© Bonacina Pierantonio

There are interior spaces that completely open up to let the outside in. These spaces challenge pre-conceived ideas, refusing to be categorized. The "indoor" and "outdoor" concepts presented in this chapter depend on one's point of view and can be refuted at any moment. These situations are quite common in houses surrounded by nature and impressive views. They are often extremely tall spaces with sliding windows that open up completely and dissolve the room's boundaries. Thus, the roof almost becomes a huge projecting element without columns or supporting walls, underneath which a whole new area is revealed, connected through furniture and lighting.

These transformations usually take place in the home's social areas, such as the dining and living rooms, and are often equipped with furniture or objects that can be used indoors or outdoors. These houses enjoy an enviable amount of light and this symbiosis with the surroundings generates sustainable air conditioning systems: large openings let air circulate throughout the house in summer, cooling it down during the hottest times of the day; in the winter, the house is warmed throughout the day when the heat accumulates in order to combat the cold nights.

CHAPTER

6

Frontier

700 Palms Residence

This house in the heart of Venice, Los Angeles, has been designed around the site's existing trees, which "were here first". The architect-owner designed three patios: one in the front (the tree patio), a second patio that is shared with the guest house, and a third patio next to the pool. Large glass surfaces allow the house to be completely opened to the exterior, while the use of weather-resistant materials or textured elements help bring the space in contact with nature, a typical feature of modernist Californian architecture.

p. 261 The barriers between the interior and exterior have been dissolved in this house, creating flexible spaces in which to enjoy the mild southern Californian climate.

House in the Jungle

The aim of this house was to create interiors that are in total synergy with the exterior. Two large symmetrical cubes embrace a central open space with 36 ft floor-to-ceiling glass windows on both ends, which helps bring the outside in. In an attempt to blend in with the beautiful surroundings, Cumaru wood paneling, running from top to bottom, extends throughout the house. The absence of partitions increases the house's integration with its surroundings and adds a spectacular element to the minimalist interiors, where the white walls are devoid of paintings.

p. 263 The simple and symmetrical style of this house contrasts with the lush jungle that surrounds it, making it easier to let nature in.

p. 267 A sleek, utilitarian white kitchen table in the main living area is mimicked by an outdoor wooden dining table which is linked to a barbecue on the shaded side of the deck.

p. 269 A large terrace bordering the house is both a place from which to observe the surrounding rain forest and a separation between nature and the building.

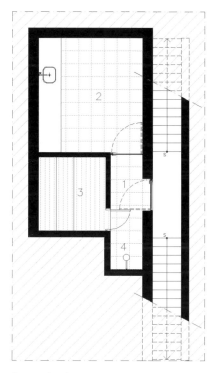

Basement floor plan

1. Basement acces
2. Storge
3. Sauna
4. Shower

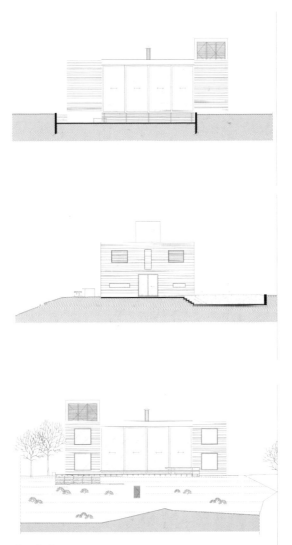

Cross Sections

Palm Beach House

This house, designed as a family vacation home and a potential permanent residence, sits on an extraordinary site facing the Australian capital's famous Palm Beach. The aim of this project was to create a seamless connection between the interior and exterior. A completely transparent home is created through large operable glazed openings and dramatic cantilevered roofs, encapsulating the spectacular panoramic views toward the north. To the south (the rear of the house), a sheltered courtyard with a pond provides a more intimate setting as well as refuge from the street.

p. 276-277 Cantilevered roofs extend over the living areas on the lower level and create shaded spaces for exterior living and dining.

Baleia House

The proposal for this home, situated on a narrow 6,243 sq ft site, was to create an extensive living space with many openings for illumination and ventilation as well as privacy from the adjacent condominiums. Thus, there are few solid façades. The house is distributed over three levels, starting with the service area, which sinks halfway into the terrain. The main level, with the living room and two bedrooms, is completely transparent, without any limits between the interior and exterior.

p. 282 A private internal garden is contained within the two blocks of all the living areas. As there are no boundaries between indoors and outdoors, the two spaces blend effortlessly.

278

Openhouse

Embedded on a narrow and sharply sloping site, this house in the famous Hollywood Hills is both integrated into the landscape and open to the sprawling city below. All boundaries between indoors and out are erased through the use of sliding glass panels on all front, side, and rear elevations of this house that open to reveal two levels of gardens and terraces. Glass is the primary material chosen for the wall enclosure: there are forty-four sliding glass panels, each 7' × 10' high, that are configured to disappear into hidden pockets or to slide beyond the building perimeter.

p. 287 Epoxy quartz flooring is used throughout the house, decks, and terraces to create a feeling of continuity between indoor and outdoor materials.

p. 288-289 Mirror plate walls—glass in the form of fixed clear plate panels—bring the views inside while mirror glass panels lend lightness to the interior spaces.

p. 290 Retaining walls are configured to extend the first floor living level into the hillside and to create a garden terrace for the second level.

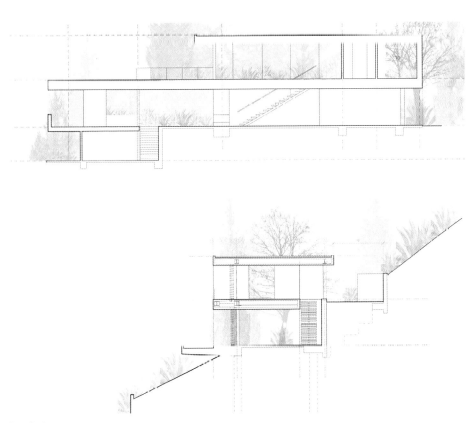

Cross Sections

Accessories Gallery

© B&B Italia

© Jane Hawley Wells

© Extremis

© Poulain & Proust

© Jane Hawley Wells

© Jane Hawley Wells

© Jane Hawley Wells

© Jane Hawley Wells

© Christophe Pillet

© Gervasoni

© Sutherland

© Sutherland

DIRECTORY OF ARCHITECTS

Arthur Casas
105 Madison Avenue
New York, NY 10016, USA
P +1 212 889 5014
Rua Capivari, 160, Pacaembu, São
Paulo, SP, Brazil
Cep: 01246-020
P+55 11 2182 7500
arthurcasas.com
House in the Jungle

Baumraum
Roonstr. 49, 28203
Bremen, Germany
P +49 (0) 4 21 70 51 22
www.baumraum.de
Between Alder and Oak
Between Magnolia and Pine

Belzberg Architects
1501 Colorado Ave, Cuite.B
Santa Mónica, California 90404, USA
P +1 310 453 0611
www.belzbergarchitects.com
Skyline Residence

Ben Bensley Design Studios
7 Sukhumvit 61, Sukhumvit Rd.
Klongton Nua, Wattana
Bangkok 10110, Thailand
P + 66 2 381 6305
www.bensley.com
Camp Howie House
Chiang Mai

Bernardes + Jacobsen
Arquitetura
Rua Corcovado casa 250
Jardim Botânico - RJ - Brazil
CEP 22460-050
P +55 11 2512 7743
www.bernardesjacobsen.com.br
Baleia House

Callas Shortridge Architects
3621 Hayden Avenue
Culver City, California 90232, USA
P +1 310 280 0404
www.callas-shortridge.com
Venice Garden

Coop Himmelb(L)au
Spengergasse 37 A
1050 Vienna, Austria
P +43 (0) 1 546 60 334
www.coop-himmelblau.at
Villa Soravia

Craig Steely Architecture
8 Beaver Street
San Francisco, CA 94114, USA
P +1 415 864 7013
www.craigsteely.com
Beaver Street Reprise

Design King
Unit 102, 21 Alberta Street
Sydney, NSW 2000, Australia
P +1161 2 9261 3062
www.designking.com.au
Palm Beach House

Diego Montero
Ruta 10 y 18 de Julio
Manantiales, Uruguay
P +598 42 77 4209
www.diegomontero.com
Hidden Paradise
Maritime Refuge

Earth Inc.
507 King Street E #112
Toronto, Canada
P +1 416 216 0378
www.earthinc.com
Princess Margaret

297

F3 Arquitectos
Ernesto Pinto Lagarrigue, 156 of. F
Bellavista-Santiago, Chile
P +56 2 735 0417
www.ftres.cl
Cachagua House

Hariri & Hariri Architecture
39 West 29th Street, 12th Floor
New York, NY 10001, USA
P +1 212 727 0338 ext. 13
www.haririandhariri.com
Wilton Pool House

Ibarra Rosano Design Architects
2849 East Sylvia Street
Tucson, Arizona 85716, USA
P +1 520 795 5477
ibarrarosano.com
Winter Residence

Isay Weinfeld
Rua Andres Fernandes 175
04536.020
São Paulo, Brazil
P+55 11 3079 7581
www.isayweinfeld.com
Iporanga

JM Architecture
Viale Monte Grappa, 2
20124, Milan, Italy
P +39 02 36565846
www.jma.it
Dolomites House

Jun Ueno
P.O. Box 4364
Palos Verdes, CA 90274, USA
P +1 310 702 560
www.magicboxincusa.com
Magic Box

LAR / Fernando Romero
Gral. Fco. Ramírez 5b Col.
Ampliación Daniel Garza
México D.F. 11840
P +52 55 2614 1060 ext.109
www.lar-fernandoromero.com
Ixtapa House

Leone Design Studio
55 Washington Street, Suite 253 B
Brooklyn New York, NY 11201, USA
P +1 718 243 9088
www.leonedesignstudio.com
A&A Outdoors

Marcio Kogan
Al. Tietê, 505, Sao Paulo, Brazil
P +55 11 308 13522
www.marciokogan.com.br
Mirindiba House

Marmol Radziner + Associates
12210 Nebraska Avenue
Los Angeles, CA 90025, USA
P +1 310 826 6222
www.marmol-radziner.com
Desert House
Isabel Trust

Martín Gómez Arquitectos
Ruta 10, Km 161
La Barra, Maldonado, Uruguay
P +598 42 772004
www.martingomezarquitectos.com
Wood Appeal

**Milagros Loitegui y Maria Silvia
Loitegui**
Esmeralda 1180 5 A, C1007ABP
Capital Federal, Buenos Aires
Argentina
P +54 911 4477 5947
Pool House

Oppenheim Architecture + Design
245 NE 37th Street
Miami, Florida 33137, USA
P +1 305 576 84 04
www.oppenoffice.com
Villa Allegra

Paul Archer Architects
3D2 Zetland House, 5-25 Scrutton St.
EC2A 4HJ, London, UK
P +44 20 7729 2729
King Henry's Road

Rios Clementi Hale Studios
639 N Larchmont Blvd
Los Angeles, CA 90004, USA
P +1 323 785 1800
www.rchstudios.com
Somer Tea House

Russell Cletta
P +1 818 225 0802
rclotta@estate-gardens.com
Calming retreat in California

Sculp(IT)Architecten Vof
Huikstraat 47
2000 Antwerp, Belgium
P +32 3 289 07 24
www.sculp.it
Bath on the rooftop

Sebastian Mariscal Studio
4125 Sorrento Valley Blvd. Suite C
San Diego, CA 92121, USA
P +1 858 558 2100 ext.118
www.sebastianmariscal.com
2inns
Six

Spaces & Places/James Craig
P +11 61 9808 5186
www.spacesandplaces.com.au
Balinese Garden

Stanley Saitowitz I Natoma Architects
1022 Natoma Street #3
San Francisco, CA 94103, USA
P +1 415 626 8977 ext. 104
www.saitowitz.co
Bridge House

Steven Erlich
10865 Washington Boulevard
Culver City, CA 90232, USA
P +1 310 838 9700
www.s-ehrlich.com
700 Palms Residence

Steven Lombardi Architect
5035.5 Newport Ave.
San Diego, CA 92107, USA
P +1 619 523 4722
www.stevenlombardi.com
Neptune

XTEN Architecture
201 S. Santa Fe Avenue, Suite 202
Los Angeles, CA 90012, USA
P +1 213 625 7002
www.xtenarchitecture.com
Openhouse

BRAND DIRECTORY

B&B Italia
www.bebitalia.it

Bonacina Pierantonio
www.bonacinapierantonio.it

Christophe Pillet
www.christophepillet.com

Conmoto
www.conmoto.com

Emme Group
www.emmegroupdesign.com

Extremis
www.extremis.be

Garpa
www.garpa.co.uk

Gervasoni
www.gervasoni1882.it

Gandía Blasco
www.gandiablasco.com

Habitat
www.habitat.net

Jane Hamley Wells
www.janehamleywells.com

Kalamazoo Outdoors Gourmet
www.kalamazoogourmet.com

Linx Professional Grills
www.lynxgrills.com

Marcel Wanders
www.marcelwanders.com

Poulain & Proust
www.poulainproust.com

Radius design
www.radius-design.com

Roche Bobois
www.roche-bobois.com

Shady Lady Lightning
www.shadyladylighting.com

Studio Lilica
www.studiolilica.com

Sutherland
www.sutherlandteak.com

Viteo
www.viteo.at